# The Comden & Green Songbook

## Betty Comden and Adolph Green

Images courtesy of the estate of Betty Comden-Kyle
and the collections of Phyllis Newman Green and Margaret A. Styne.

**Alfred**

Produced by
Alfred Music Publishing Co., Inc.
P.O. Box 10003
Van Nuys, CA 91410-0003
alfred.com

Printed in USA.

ISBN-10: 0-7390-6492-4
ISBN-13: 978-0-7390-6492-4

# Contents

# Words and More Words
## Betty Comden and Adolph Green

As the longest surviving writing team in Broadway history, Betty Comden (1917–2006) and Adolph Green (1914–2002) were professional partners for over a half-century. The team was unusual in several regards: as a man and a woman working closely together for decades, both were married to other people. They were also one of the few successful songwriting teams that only wrote lyrics. (Others in this short list include 1920s writers B. G. DeSylva and Lew Brown and the husband-and-wife team of Alan and Marilyn Bergman.) Their style was chiefly comedic, although they were also capable of writing lyrics that were wistful ("The Party's Over"), philosophical ("Comes Once in a Lifetime"), and magical ("Never Never Land"). What best typifies a Comden and Green lyric is that it is nearly always tightly and inextricably woven into the fabric of the stories and characters it was written for. Their lyrics also reflect much about who Comden and Green were, exuding wit, humor, intelligence, exuberance, and joie de vivre.

The Revuers. Left to right: Adolph Green, John Frank, Betty Comden, Alvin Hammer, Judy Holliday.

They collaborated with some of the finest composers in the Broadway and film worlds, including Leonard Bernstein, Jule Styne, Cy Coleman, André Previn, Morton Gould, Saul Chaplin, and Roger Edens. Many of their songs remain timeless standards today.

Adolph Green was born in the Bronx to a family of Hungarian immigrants. In 1937, while attending a summer camp, he became friends with a young music counselor named Leonard Bernstein. Green met Betty Comden (born Elizabeth Cohen in New York) in 1938 when both were undergraduates at New York University and looking for theatrical agents to represent them. Along with a friend, Judy Tuvim (who anglicized her surname to Holliday), they formed a cabaret act called the Revuers: with Alvin Hammer and John Frank rounding out the group, they began an engagement at the Village Vanguard in Greenwich Village. By then, Bernstein had graduated from Harvard and often could be seen pounding the piano during the Revuers' act at the Vanguard as well as at the classier Blue Angel club farther uptown.

In 1944, Bernstein asked Comden and Green to work with him on a musical theatre version of his ballet *Fancy Free*. The result was *On the Town*, Comden and Green's first hit, which featured such memorable songs as "New York, New York," "Some Other Time," and "Lucky to Be Me." For this show, they actually wrote themselves into the script, with each playing key roles. Green was Ozzie, one of three sailors on leave in New York, and Comden played his paramour, anthropologist Clair de Loone.

Leonard Bernstein, composer of *On the Town*, flanked by Betty Comden and Adolph Green.

From then on, Comden and Green became a force on the Broadway scene, and soon expanded their talents to Hollywood, writing material for successful films such as *Good News*, *Singin' in the Rain*, and *The Band Wagon*. They worked on one more Broadway show with Bernstein (*Wonderful Town*), but their longest and most prolific partnership was with composer Jule Styne. This collaboration began with the musical revue *Two on the Aisle* and continued with the Broadway hits *Bells Are Ringing*, *Do Re Mi*, and *Peter Pan*. All told, Comden, Green, and Styne worked on nine productions as a team. Comden and Green's careers as performers culminated in 1958 with the highly acclaimed show *A Party with Betty Comden and Adolph Green*, in which they performed songs and sketches from their shows, films, and night club act with the Revuers. (*A Party* was revived in 1977.)

Despite changing times and tastes, the 1960s saw Comden and Green continue their career, penning lyrics for the film *What a Way to Go* and shows such as *Fade Out–Fade In*, and *Hallelujah, Baby!* In 1978, they worked with composer Cy Coleman on what many consider to be the last of the great classic Broadway musicals,

*On the Twentieth Century*. Their last show together, again with Coleman, came in 1991 with *The Will Rogers Follies*. During their long career together, Comden and Green won a total of seven Tony® awards and were elected to the Songwriters Hall of Fame. In 1991, they were awarded the prestigous Kennedy Center Honors.

In private life, Betty Comden was married to businessman Steven Kyle from 1942 until his death in 1979. Of Adolph Green's three marriages, his most successful was to actress Phyllis Newman, who he married in 1960. They remained together until his death in 2002. Ms. Newman understudied Judy Holliday in *Bells Are Ringing* and was a featured performer in *Subways Are for Sleeping*.

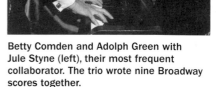

Betty Comden and Adolph Green with Jule Styne (left), their most frequent collaborator. The trio wrote nine Broadway scores together.

# About the Songs

In compiling this songbook, we were fortunate to have the assistance of Ms. Newman, who recommended many of the songs that were selected. Four songs were chosen from Comden and Green's breakthrough show, *On the Town* (1944). "New York, New York" has become an iconic tribute to the bustling Big Apple, with its mantra, "The Bronx is up and the Battery's down / The people ride in a hole in the ground." Some things never change. "Lonely Town" is sung by lovestruck sailor Gabey (John Battles), who becomes infatuated with the image of "Miss Turnstiles" that he sees on the subway. After spending much of the first act looking for her, he finds her, his mood brightens, and he sings "Lucky to Be Me" while awaiting her arrival in Times Square. "Some Other Time" is sung by sailors Chip (Cris Alexander) and Ozzie (Adolph Green) and their newfound girlfriends, Claire (Betty Comden) and Hildy (Nancy Walker), as they realize their time together must come to an end.

"The French Lesson" was the only song written by Comden and Green (with composer Roger Edens) that appeared in the 1947 film *Good News*. The entertaining number is sung in the movie by Tait College co-ed librarian Connie Lane (June Allyson) and football star Tommy Marlowe (Peter Lawford). Tommy is flunking French and can't play in the big game unless he passes the class, so he engages Connie as his private tutor.

Comden and Green's first association with composer Jule Styne was in the musical revue *Two on the Aisle*, which made its debut during the summer of 1951. The song "If You Hadn't But You Did" is a tour de force for actress Dolores Gray, a hilarious patter song in which she lists all the reasons why she bumped off her philandering boyfriend. The lyrics utilize a run-on succession of actual and truncated words designed to rhyme with the word "if," including "whiff," "stiff," "cliff," "terrif," "hieroglyph," and "what's the diff."

At one time, Comden and Green were living bi-coastal lives, writing for the theatre in New York and periodically coming out West to work with the vaunted "Freed Unit" on the MGM lot. The celebrated MGM motion picture musical *Singin' in the Rain* came as a result of producer Arthur Freed wishing to have a film produced using songs he wrote with Nacio Herb Brown in the 1920s. Freed hired Comden and Green to come up with a story to surround the songs. The film was directed by Stanley Donen and Gene Kelly. The breezy screenplay features one non-Freed/Brown song, with lyrics by Comden and Green and music by MGM house composer/arranger Roger Edens. Titled "Moses," the song is an exercise in tongue-twisting, sung by silent screen star Don Lockwood (Gene Kelly) and best buddy Cosmo Brown (Donald O'Connor) to their stupefied diction teacher. The sequence culminates in an electrifying dance routine by Kelly and O'Connor. *Singin' in the Rain* is now considered to be the greatest film musical of all time.

Comden and Green with Gene Kelly, who worked with them on two films: *Singin' in the Rain* (1951) and *It's Always Fair Weather* (1955).

In 1953, Comden and Green reunited with Leonard Bernstein for another Broadway musical, *Wonderful Town*, based on Ruth McKenny's novel *My Sister Eileen*. In the song "Ohio," sisters Ruth (Rosalind Russell) and Eileen (Edith Adams), who have just arrived in New York, regret leaving their comfortable but boring hometown. The plaintive lyrics include a patter section that colorfully describes the "stuffy" and "provincial" lifestyle that convinced them to leave for the Big Apple. In "It's Love," Eileen makes magazine story editor Bob Baker (George Gaynes) realize that he's in love with her sister Ruth. The score for the show won Comden and Green their first of seven Tony awards.

Peter Pan (1954) is one of the few Broadway musicals that needed punching up from a second team of songwriters. In this case, Comden, Green, and Jule Styne were brought onboard to enhance the score by Moose Charlap and Carolyn Leigh after the show's opening on the West Coast. By the time it reached Broadway, the show featured a handful of the trio's most delightful songs. The enchanting "Never Never Land" is sung by Peter (Mary Martin) in describing his otherworldly island home to the impressionable Wendy (Kathy Nolan). In "Captain Hook's Waltz," the lugubrious pirate captain (Cyril Ritchard) reveals that underneath his wicked, nefarious skin he's just as insidious as on the outside ("Who's the crawlingest, cruelist, crummiest, crookedest crook?").

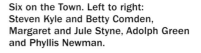

Six on the Town. Left to right: Steven Kyle and Betty Comden, Margaret and Jule Styne, Adolph Green and Phyllis Newman.

For the MGM film musical It's Always Fair Weather (1955), Comden and Green were again invited to collaborate with director Stanley Donen and Gene Kelly. The story was designed to be a sequel to On the Town, with three ex-G.I.'s reuniting ten years after serving together in World War II. The most celebrated sequence occurs when Kelly sings "I Like Myself" while roller-skating on the busy streets of New York. André Previn wrote the melody to Comden and Green's lyrics.

The delightful Broadway musical Bells Are Ringing reunited Comden and Green with their former Revuers partner Judy Holliday, who was making her musical comedy debut. Jule Styne composed the music for the show, in which Holliday played Ella Peterson, a telephone answering service operator who lives vicariously through the relationships of her customers. Eventually, she begins to meddle more than she should and falls in love with aspiring playwright Jeff Moss (Sydney Chaplin), the two singing the romantic duet "Long Before I Knew You" and one of Comden and Green's most celebrated lyrics,

The stars and composers of Hallelujah, Baby! (1967). Left to right (standing): Adolph Green, Betty Comden, Leslie Uggams, Robert Hooks, Allen Case, Barbara Sharma. Seated at the piano is Jule Styne.

"Just in Time." Later, after attending a party where she feels she doesn't fit in, Ella believes her love affair with Jeff has ended and sings the wistful "The Party's Over."

After working on Say, Darling in 1958, the Comden/Green/Styne triumvirate's next Broadway show was Do Re Mi, which starred Phil Silvers as a different kind of operator. In the show, Silvers played small-timer Hubie Cram, who is always on the lookout for a get-rich-quick scheme. He finds one in the juke box business, but runs afoul of the underworld and soon finds himself in over his head. A secondary story develops when waitress Tilda Mullen (Nancy Dussault) falls instantly in love with polished record producer John Henry Wheeler (John Reardon), and they sing the duet "Fireworks." As a former Tin Pan Alley songsmith, Jule Styne usually tried to insert what he thought would be a hit pop song into his shows, and "Make Someone Happy" had all the earmarks of a classic. As soon as Comden and Green finished the lyrics, Styne knew the song was "gold record" material. The optimistic message song was sung by Reardon in the show and has recently been recorded by Barbra Streisand.

Another song of advice comes in the show Subways Are for Sleeping, which Comden and Green wrote with Styne in 1961. The show's plot surrounds magazine writer Angie McKay (Carol Lawrence), who seeks to write a story about how a faction of New York City's homeless population lives. "Comes Once in a Lifetime" is sung by Angie and Tom Bailey (Sydney Chaplin), a well-dressed drifter who acts as a one-man employment agency for other disenfranchised street dwellers. They sing the song as they explore the French Wing of the Metropolitan Museum; the song's basic message is to take life one day at a time ("While the future waits, the present swings!"). Dressed as a street corner Santa Claus, Bailey also sings "Be a Santa," which has the effect of an inspirational gospel number on his fellow charity Santas.

Fade Out–Fade In (1964), with a score also written by Comden, Green, and Styne, was a vehicle for the comedic talents of Carol Burnett. Burnett played an aspiring actress in the 1930s named Hope Springfield. "You Mustn't Be Discouraged" is a sprightly number sung by Hope and actor Lou Williams (Tiger Haynes), as they do impressions of 1930s film stars Shirley Temple and Bill "Bojangles" Robinson, including the famous "stair dance" from The Little Colonel.

Social consciousness was in vogue in the 1960s music scene, and Broadway was no exception. Hallelujah, Baby! deals with the struggle for equality by African Americans in the first half of the 20th century. The show made a star of Leslie Uggams, who played Georgina, a servant who is determined to have her own home and her own life ("My Own Morning"). Georgina's dream is to be a success in show business, and her soaring lament "Being Good Isn't Good Enough" helped earn Uggams a Tony for Best Actress in a Musical. The score also won a Tony that year; it was the second for Comden and Green as lyricists and the first for Jule Styne as composer. The rhythmic "When the Weather's Better," which was cut from the show, is featured for the first time in this songbook.

This rehearsal photo from the original Broadway production of On the Twentieth Century was presented as an opening night gift by director Harold Prince. Left to right: Adolph Green, Prince, Betty Comden, Imogene Coca, John Cullum, Madeline Kahn, composer Cy Coleman, choreographer Larry Fuller.

Comden and Green's fourth Tony (their third was for Applause in 1970, for which they wrote the book only) was won for On the Twentieth Century (1978). That show featured music by Cy Coleman, with whom they had previously worked on the revue Straws in the Wind, directed by Phyllis Newman. On the Twentieth Century combines the feel of a comic opera with a storyline that harkens back to the days of 1930s screwball film comedies. The uplifting title song is sung by the passengers onboard the luxurious 20th Century Limited, on its way to New York City.

Although A Doll's Life did not find its audience, its score, with lyrics by Comden and Green and music by Larry Grossman, nevertheless was nominated for a Tony for Best Original Score. "Learn to Be Lonely" is a thought-provoking soliloquy sung by Nora (Betsy Joslyn), who has left her husband and is now learning to live independently.

Betty and Adolph in 1977, during the revival of A Party with Betty Comden and Adolph Green.

Comden and Green's final Broadway show was the flashy, pull-all-the-stops-out tribute to humorist Will Rogers, one of the most colorful figures in American history. The Will Rogers Follies (1991) featured all the trappings of classic Broadway: high-kicking chorus girls, razzle-dazzle production numbers, and top-notch songs written by Comden, Green, and Cy Coleman. The song "Look Around" is a low-key respite to the gaudy proceedings, in which Comden and Green mask an ecological message in a cloak of nostalgia. "Never Met a Man I Didn't Like" adapts Will Rogers's most famous quote and turns it into an anthem and the show's closing number. With The Will Rogers Follies, Betty Comden and Adolph Green closed their long Broadway career in style, winning their fifth Tony for Best Original Score.

Betty Comden and Adolph Green's body of work over six decades constitutes one of the most remarkable partnerships in show business history. The best of friends and inseparable as collaborators, their work has proved to be as timeless as the Great White Way itself. This songbook is but a small part of their indelible legacy, but serves as a grand introduction to many of their best-loved works.

## Cary Ginell
Popular Music Editor
Alfred Music Publishing Co., Inc.

# The Other Woman

Adolph and I met when I auditioned to be Judy Holliday's understudy in *Bells Are Ringing*. I was catatonically nervous knowing I would be singing and acting in front of three theatre legends—Betty Comden, Adolph Green, and Jule Styne. I got the job and I got a husband (that's a whole other songbook), and I also got to have, and be, the other woman in this, our life. I was marrying a team, and embarking on a unique adventure.

Writing and onstage, they were the perfect fit, perfect foils—Betty was dignified, still, and classy, and Adolph was always in motion, a manic sprite from another planet. They so loved to perform, but they were ambitious and uniquely talented as writers.

Offstage, Adolph and I were a perfect fit as well. We were two people who found each other completely interesting and funny, loving our lives and our children, with never a bump in the road (a complete canard). But, (a truth) we never wanted to work together, writing or onstage. As Jule Styne used to say, "Phyllis does a solo."

I did have a wonderfully varied career in TV and clubs as well as in the theatre, but our professional and personal lives did intersect at many points. For example, in 1971 there was a Broadway revival of their first show, *On The Town*. They thought I would be right for Betty's original part. Bernadette Peters and Donna McKechnie were playing the other two female leads. I thought it was a terrible idea.

Why, you ask?

Sigmund Freud would have told you that it was a no-win situation and kind of creepy. It was the first show for Comden, Green, and Leonard Bernstein. They were all in their twenties. Betty and Adolph wrote two good parts for themselves, the show was a triumph, and they had that indelible memory of every moment and every line reading. Who could compete with that, and who would want to?

Well, wife loves husband and show, and is quite flattered, so . . . know only this: the pleasure of singing "Some Other Time," one of their most beautiful songs, superseded Freud, Jung, and all the wife's show biz smarts.

Then, of course, there was *Bells Are Ringing*.

I loved watching Judy and Sydney Chaplin perform their "Just In Time" duet. It was charming and funny and sexy. When Judy sang "The Party's Over," she did it simply, purely, and truthfully, which is the way she did everything. Adolph told me that it terrified her to have to sing a ballad solo. When she sang with the Revuers, she always sang the harmony. So Betty, Adolph, and Jule tricked her by teaching her the melody as if it were the harmony. The moment she felt comfortable and sang it in character, there was that overused but apt "Aha!" moment.

For *Subways Are for Sleeping*, I had to audition five times, the last time in a towel and a blonde wig. It was the first time I ever heard of not sleeping with the author to get the part. I won a Tony.

For *Wonderful Town*, Rosalind Russell told them there were only four good notes she could sing, so the songs were tailored to suit her limited range and to take advantage of her exraordinary comedic talents.

Phyllis Newman with Orson Bean on Broadway in *Subways Are for Sleeping* (c. 1962).

When they did *Peter Pan*, Jerry Robbins called them and Jule Styne in to help after the show opened. They knew of Cyril Ritchard's wonderful insanity onstage, hence "Captain Hook's Waltz," but they also wanted to capture the essence of J.M. Barrie's glorious concept, and they did so with the deceptively simple, yet haunting, "Never Never Land."

Their shows are filled with optimism and happy endings. Their range was vast, from the zany "Moses" to the honest and heartbreaking "Learn to Be Lonely," which they wrote after Betty's husband Steve died.

As I look through these songs, I think of how many times I heard Betty and Adolph perform them: at benefits, parties, and wherever they could. Performing renewed their creative energy and their faith in themselves. It was visible and tangible, and they lit up any place they were, as if they were born with built-in spotlights.

There's a reason they called their own show *A Party*. Just picture our big living room high above Central Park, with the Steinway that Adolph bought with his first check from *On The Town* dominating the room. Look at the list of their collaborators, their stars—the talented, interesting group they worked and played with, singing or playing the piano, martinis and wit flowing. They still couldn't believe they had made it, but they had and they deserved "a party."

The other story is that Comden and Green met EVERY DAY, every single day, and worked—on a show, or an idea, or just in despair, looking for a project, "the kids trying to make good." Their songs and shows speak for themselves.

Betty was the perfect woman to be the "Other, Other Woman," and Adolph, well, he was just Adolph—my Adolph, the one and only Adolph.

So go forth and sing and play and enjoy these glorious songs, and you will "Make ~~Someone~~ Happy."

*Everyone*

**—Phyllis Newman**
(Mrs. Adolph Green)

# BE A SANTA

## (from *Subways Are for Sleeping*)

Lyrics by
BETTY COMDEN
and ADOLPH GREEN

Music by
JULE STYNE

**In a bright tempo**

*Refrain: (brisk and cheerful)*

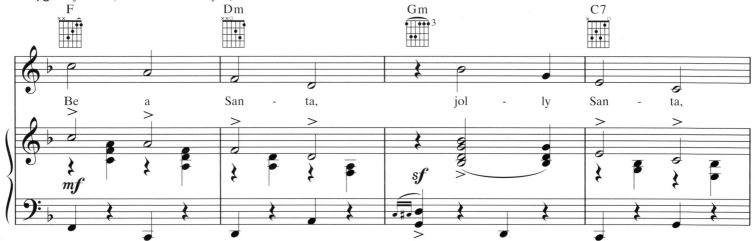

Be a San - ta, jol - ly San - ta,

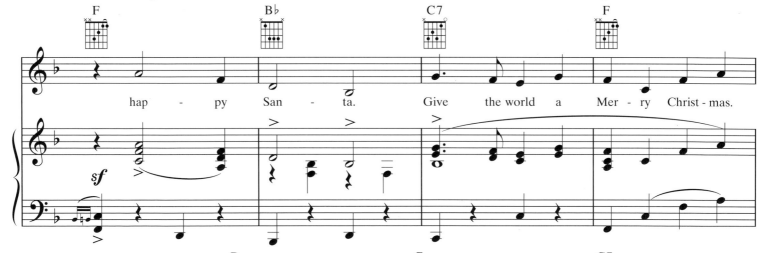

hap - py San - ta. Give the world a Mer - ry Christ - mas.

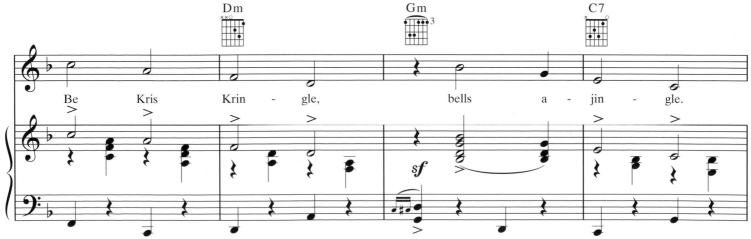

Be Kris Krin - gle, bells a - jin - gle.

11

Be so jol - ly, decked with hol - ly,

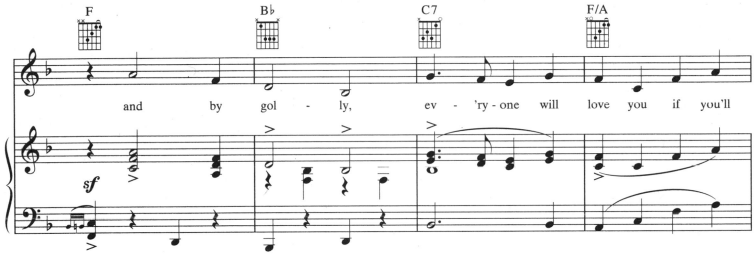

and by gol - ly, ev - 'ry-one will love you if you'll

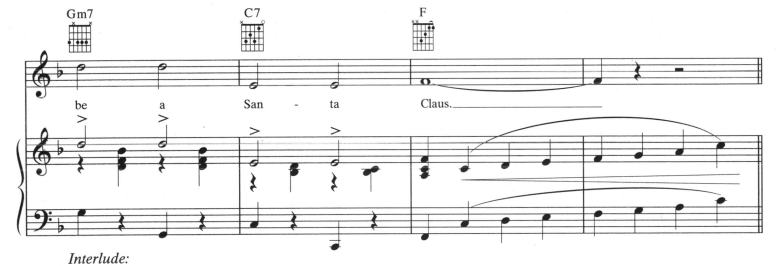

be a San - ta Claus._____

*Interlude:*

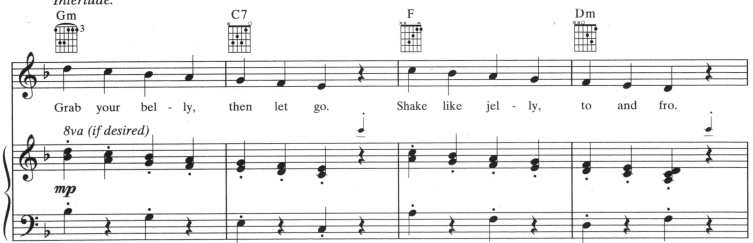

Grab your bel - ly, then let go. Shake like jel - ly, to and fro.

12

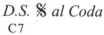

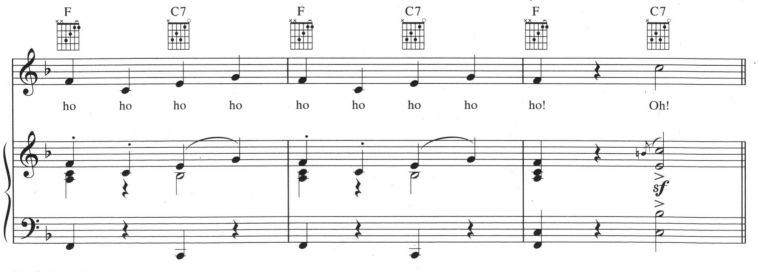

# BEING GOOD ISN'T GOOD ENOUGH

(from *Hallelujah, Baby!*)

Lyrics by
BETTY COMDEN and ADOLPH GREEN

Music by
JULE STYNE

Being Good Isn't Good Enough - 4 - 4

# CAPTAIN HOOK'S WALTZ

Lyrics by
BETTY COMDEN and ADOLPH GREEN

(from *Peter Pan*)

Music by
JULE STYNE

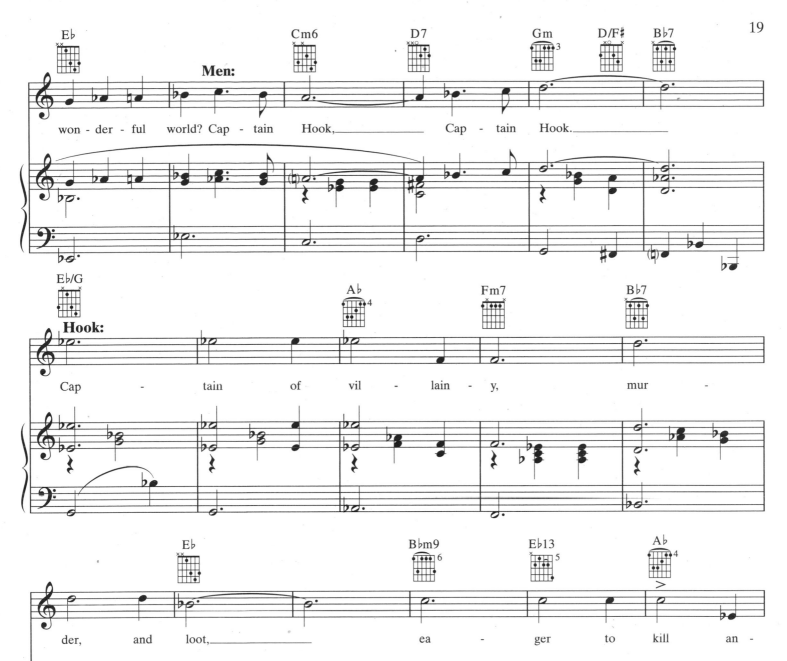

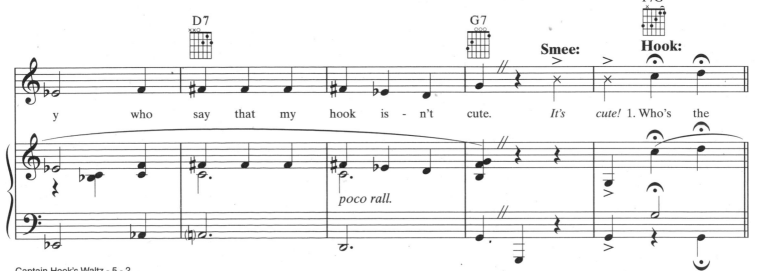

Captain Hook's Waltz - 5 - 2

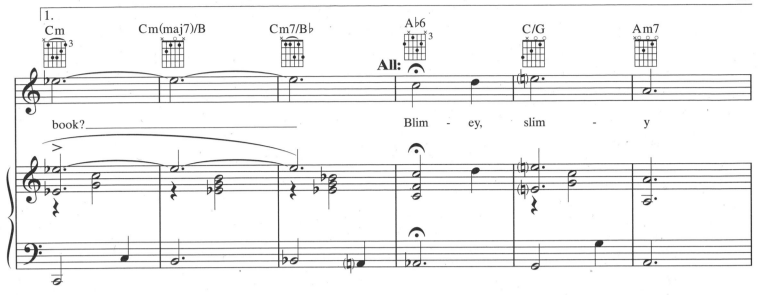

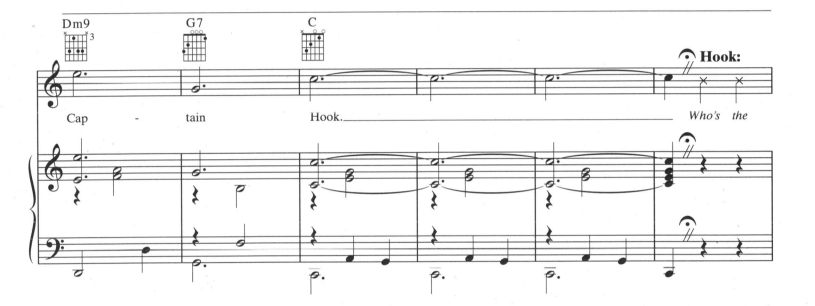

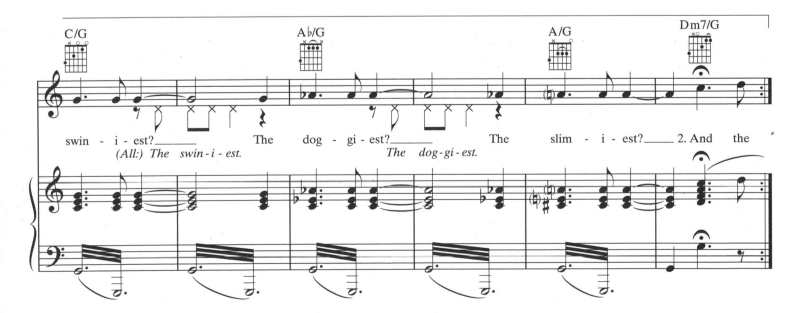

# COMES ONCE IN A LIFETIME

(from *Subways Are for Sleeping*)

Lyrics by
BETTY COMDEN and ADOLPH GREEN

Music by
JULE STYNE

Moderately

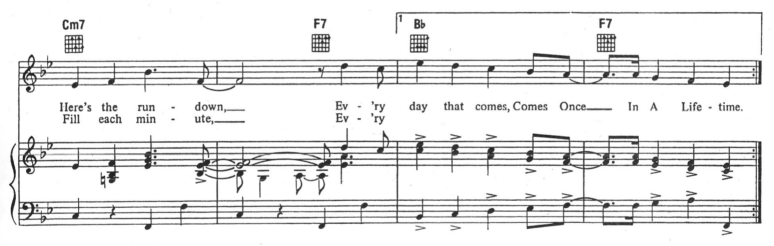

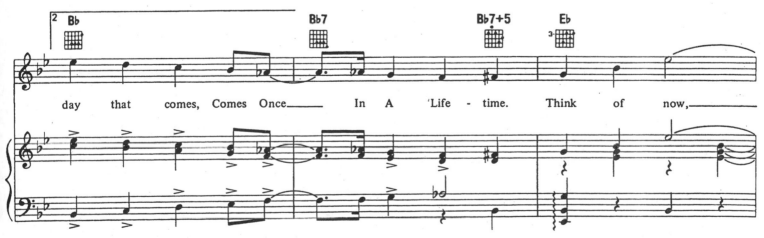

Comes Once in a Lifetime - 3 - 1

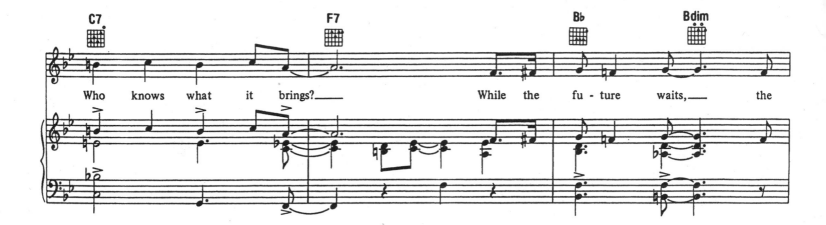

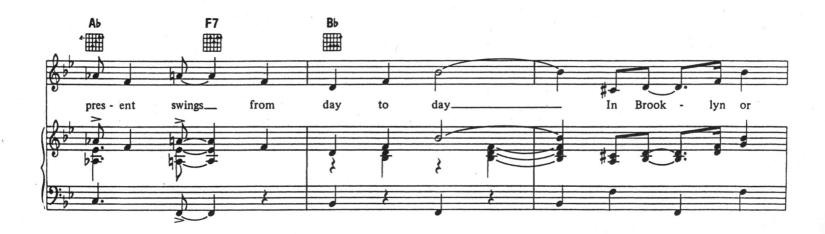

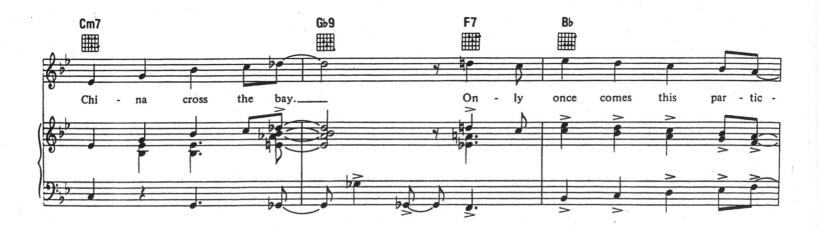

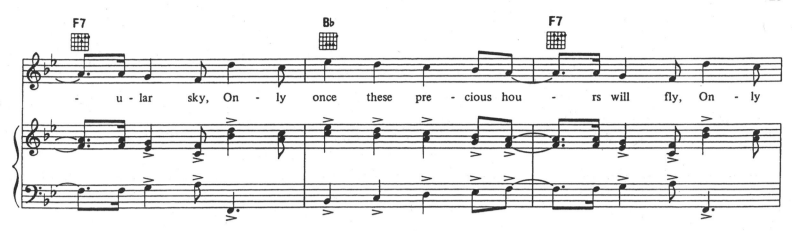

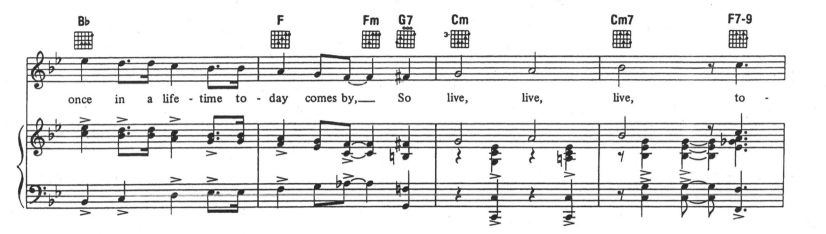

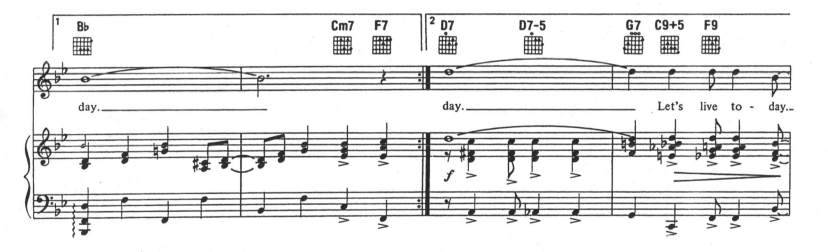

Comes Once in a Lifetime - 3 - 3

# FIREWORKS

(from *Do Re Mi*)

Lyrics by
**BETTY COMDEN and ADOLPH GREEN**

Music by
**JULE STYNE**

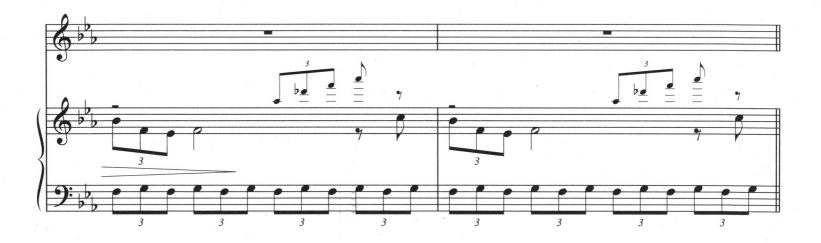

**Wheeler:**

What's this I feel?_____

**Tilda:**

What an at - trac - tive fel - low!___

28

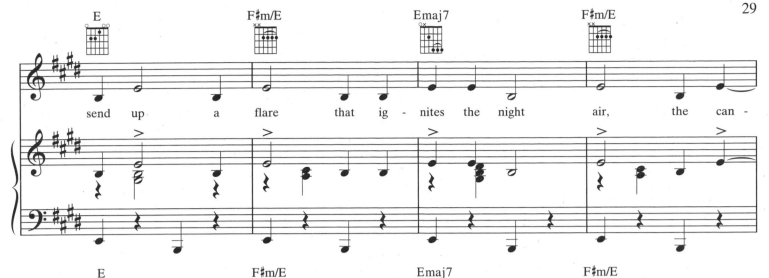

send up a flare that ig - nites the night air, the can -

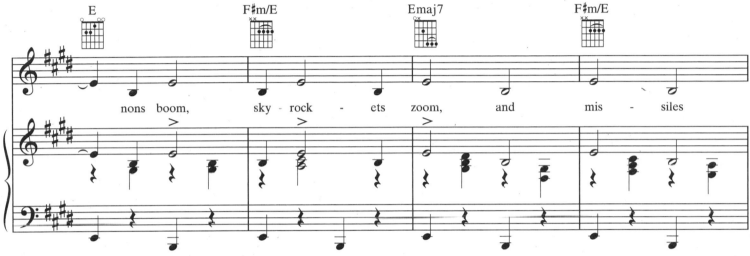

nons boom, sky - rock - ets zoom, and mis - siles

fly._____ Fi - re-works!

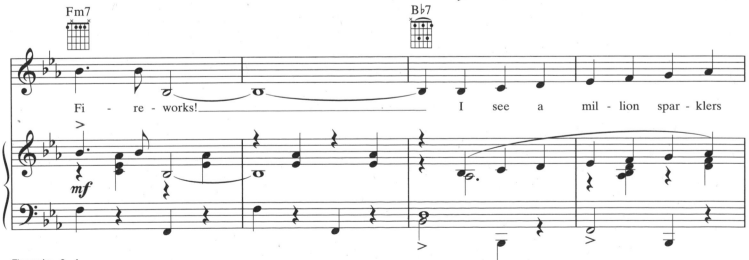

Fi - re - works!_____ I see a mil - lion spar - klers

32

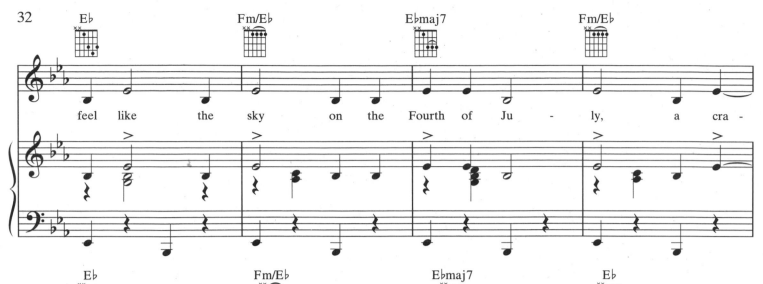

feel like the sky on the Fourth of Ju - ly, a cra -

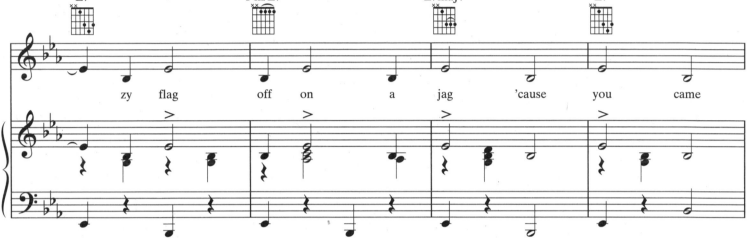

zy flag off on a jag 'cause you came

by.

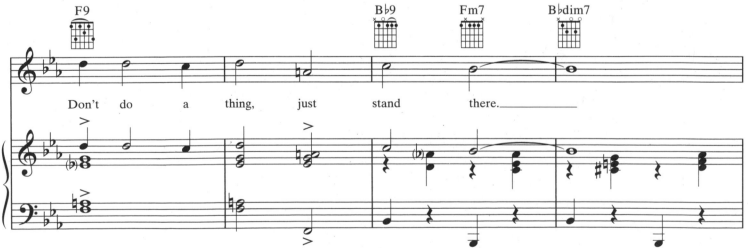

Don't do a thing, just stand there.

33

Fireworks - 9 - 8

# THE FRENCH LESSON

(from *Good News*)

Lyrics by
BETTY COMDEN and ADOLPH GREEN

Music by
ROGER EDENS

call this work! It's more like play! In no time flat, Je parle Fran -

çais.    (Spoken:) She: Had enough?    He: No, I'm just starting.    She: All right, you asked for it.    2. The

D.S. 𝄋 al Coda

⊕ Coda

porte du bois, rouge, blanc, et noir, le pa - pier, le ca - hier, le cray - on, la chaise, la plume, le liv - re.

J'ouvre    la porte,    Je ferme    la porte.    She: That's mar - vel - ous! He: My

38

The French Lesson - 6 - 4

# IF YOU HADN'T BUT YOU DID

## (from *Two on the Aisle*)

Lyrics by
BETTY COMDEN
and ADOLPH GREEN

Music by
JULE STYNE

44

I'm gon - na miss you, ba - - by,

Fm7    Fm7/B♭    Fm7    Fm7/B♭    E♭7

and I could get spe - cif. Ah! What's the diff!___

A♭m    A♭m(maj7)    A♭m7

If the best years of my life___ were - n't spent as your wife___ with no

A♭m6    A♭m    A♭m(maj7)

mar - riage cer - tif,___ If you were not such a two - tim - ing guy.__

# I LIKE MYSELF

(from *It's Always Fair Weather*)

Lyrics by
BETTY COMDEN
and ADOLPH GREEN

Music by
ANDRÉ PREVIN

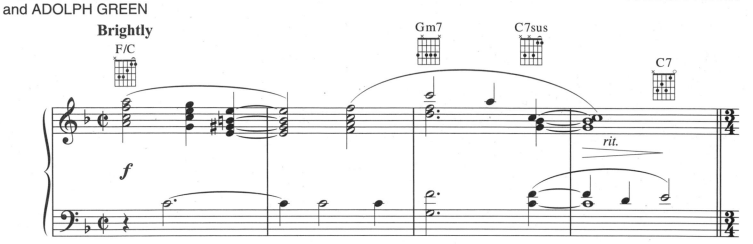

Why am I feel-ing so good?

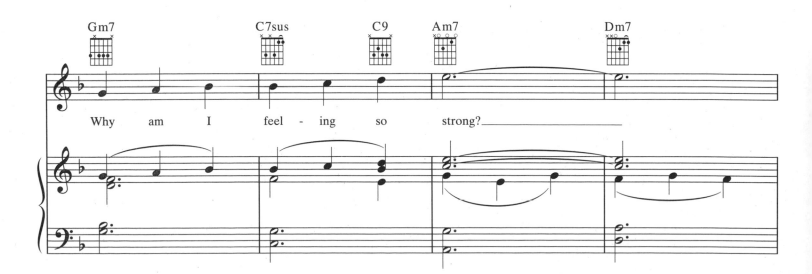

Why am I feel-ing so strong?

I Like Myself - 4 - 1

**Moderately**

*Refrain:*

# IT'S LOVE

(from *Wonderful Town*)

Lyrics by
BETTY COMDEN and ADOLPH GREEN

Music by
LEONARD BERNSTEIN

It's Love - 7 - 1

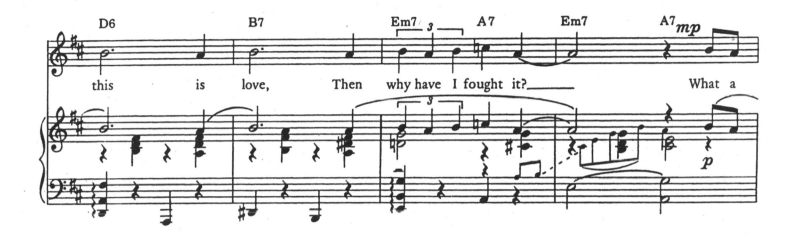

It's Love - 7 - 4

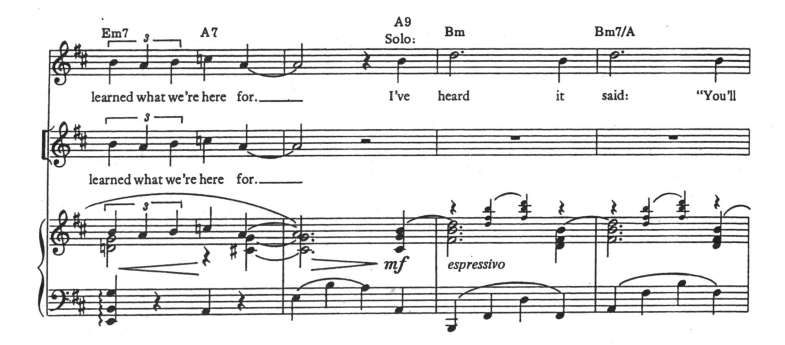

# LEARN TO BE LONELY

(from *A Doll's Life*)

Lyrics by
BETTY COMDEN and ADOLPH GREEN

Music by
LARRY GROSSMAN

Learn to Be Lonely - 7 - 1

64

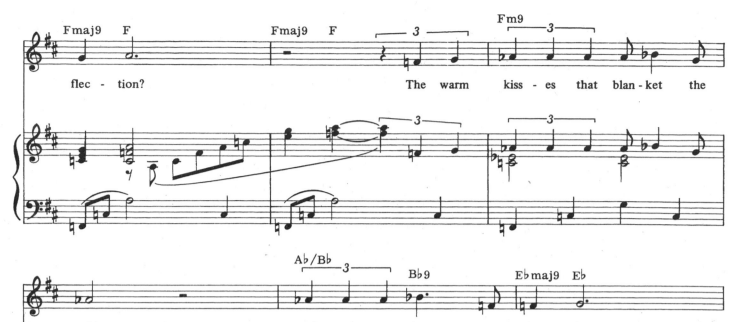

flec - tion? The warm kiss - es that blan - ket the

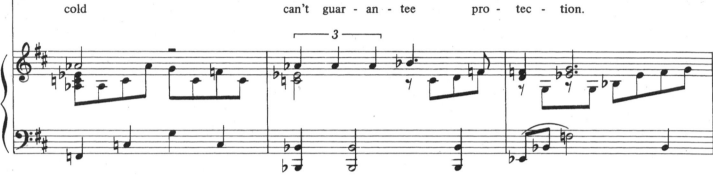

cold can't guar - an - tee pro - tec - tion.

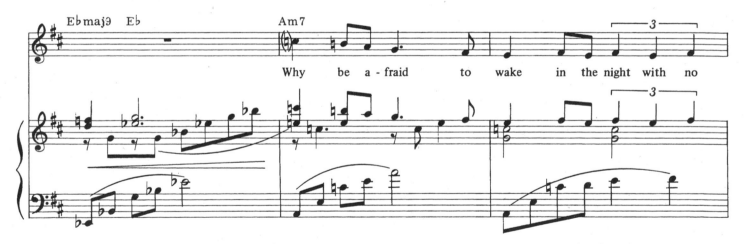

Why be a - fraid to wake in the night with no

head on the pil - low be - side you, with no hand you can reach for to

N/A

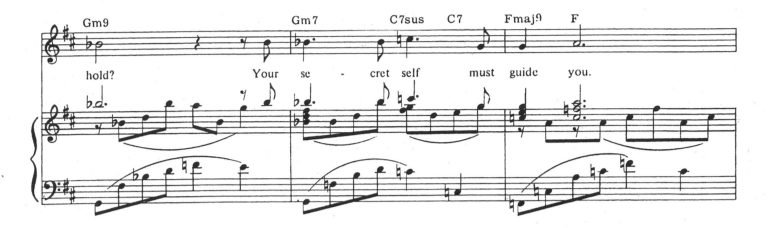

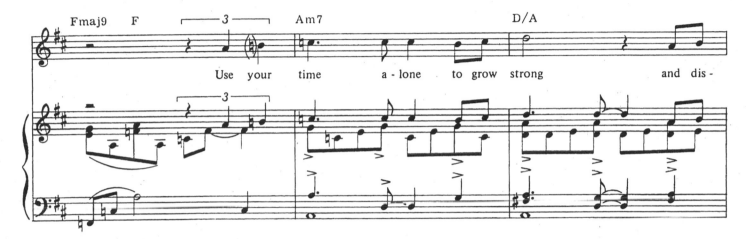

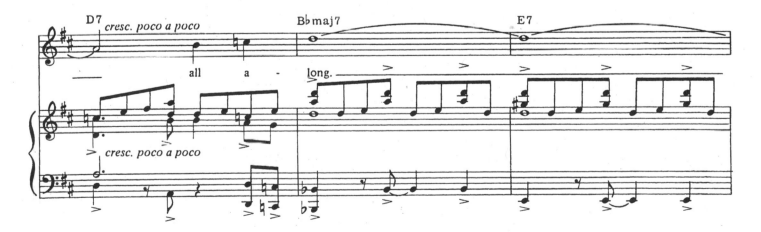

66

B9sus  B9  Gmaj9

*mf*

own  is to  mate  and feel a - lone.  You ____

Gmaj7

F#m7  Bm7  *f*  F#m9

____ are your one and on - ly ____  learn  to

*f*

Em9  N.C. *mp*

live, ____  Learn To Be

*mp*

Dmaj7

Lone  -  ly. ____

*p*

# JUST IN TIME

(from *Bells Are Ringing*)

Lyrics by
BETTY COMDEN
and ADOLPH GREEN

Music by
JULE STYNE

at._____ "There's no hope for

him," my dear-est friends would mut-ter,

I was some-thing dragged in by the cat, then...

*Refrain (with a lilt):*

Just in time,_____ I found you just in time._____ Be - fore you

*poco rall.*

doubt or fear,____ I've found my way.____ For love came

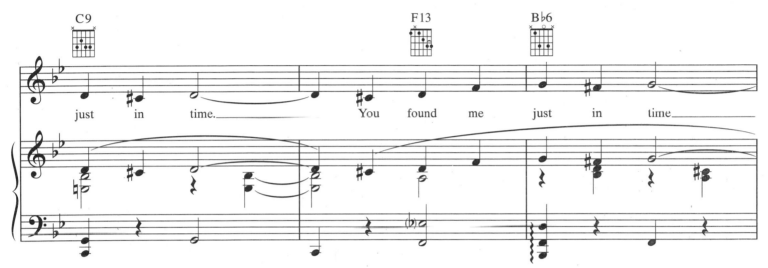

just in time.____ You found me just in time____

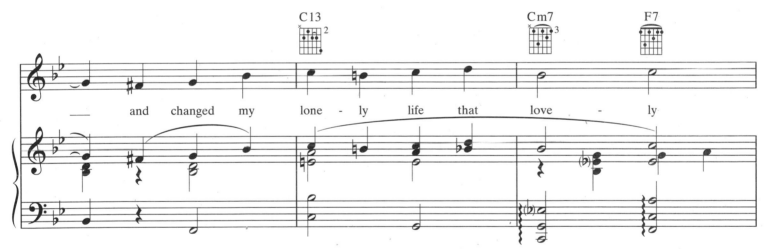

____ and changed my lone-ly life that love-ly

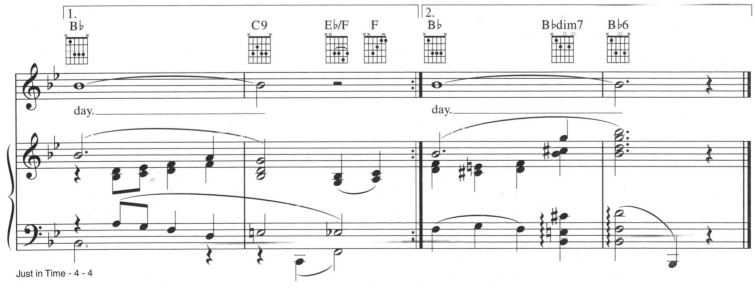

day.____ day.____

Just in Time - 4 - 4

# LONELY TOWN

(from *On the Town*)

Lyrics by
BETTY COMDEN and ADOLPH GREEN

Music by
LEONARD BERNSTEIN

Refrain:

A town's a lone-ly town when you pass through, and there is no one wait-ing there for you, then it's a lone-ly town. You wan-der up and down, the crowds rush by; a mil-lion fac-es pass be-fore your

# LONG BEFORE I KNEW YOU

(from *Bells Are Ringing*)

Lyrics by
BETTY COMDEN and ADOLPH GREEN

Music by
JULE STYNE

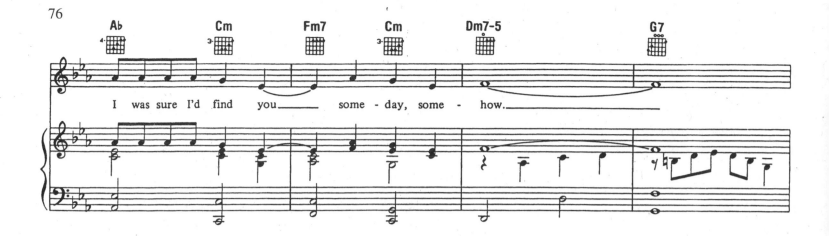

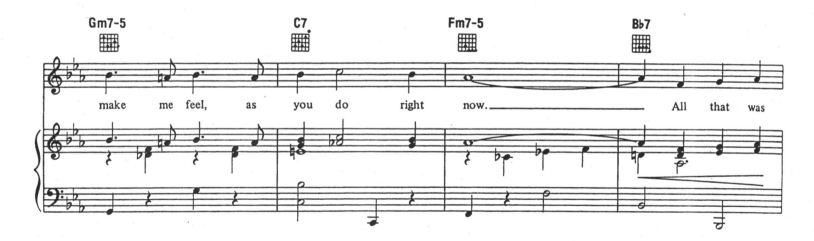

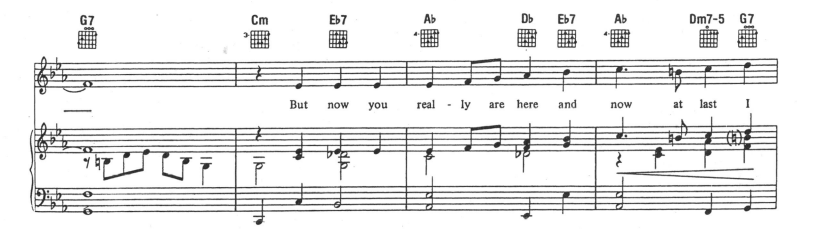

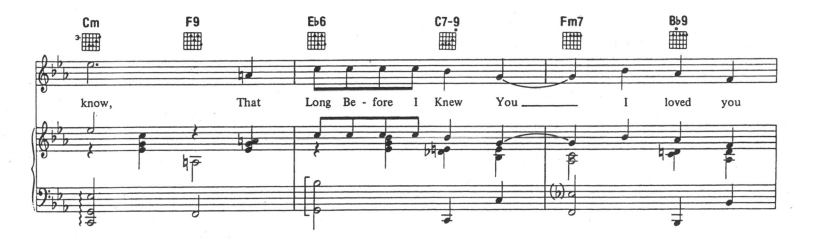

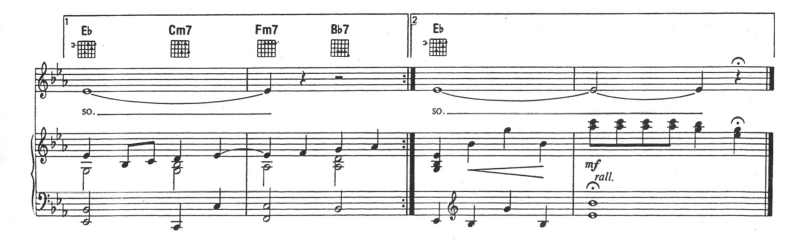

# LOOK AROUND

(from *The Will Rogers Follies*)

Music by
CY COLEMAN

Lyrics by
BETTY COMDEN and ADOLPH GREEN

Look Around - 3 - 1

# MAKE SOMEONE HAPPY
### (from *Do Re Mi*)

Lyrics by
BETTY COMDEN
and ADOLPH GREEN

Music by
JULE STYNE

# LUCKY TO BE ME

(from *On the Town*)

Lyrics by
BETTY COMDEN and ADOLPH GREEN

Music by
LEONARD BERNSTEIN

# MY OWN MORNING

(from *Hallelujah, Baby!*)

Lyrics by
BETTY COMDEN and ADOLPH GREEN

Music by
JULE STYNE

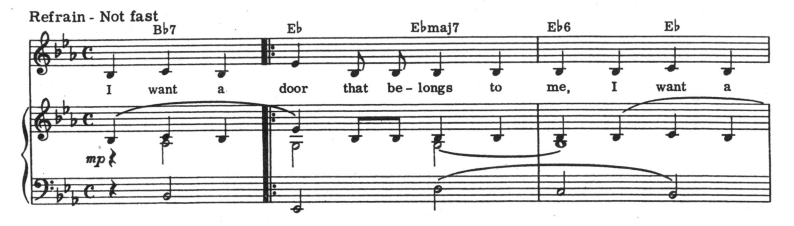

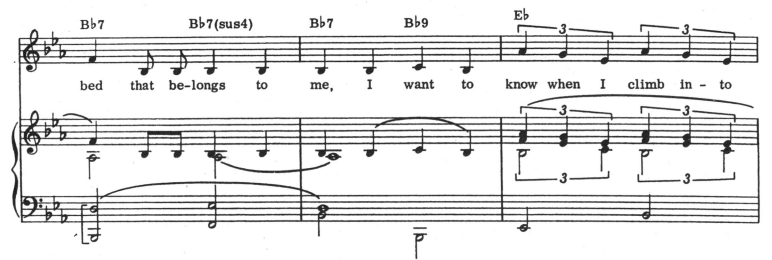

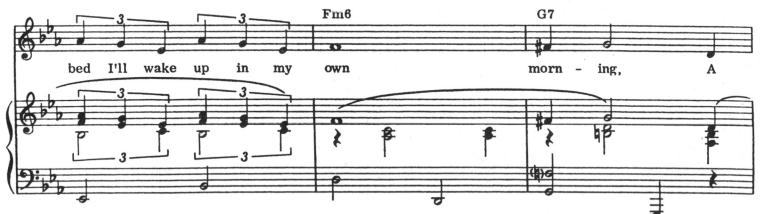

My Own Morning - 4 - 3

# MOSES
### (from *Singin' in the Rain*)

Lyrics by
BETTY COMDEN
and ADOLPH GREEN

Music by
ROGER EDENS

Mo - ses sup - pos - es his toes - es are ros - es, but Mo - ses sup - pos - es er -

ro - ne - ous - ly.___ But Mo - ses, he knows - es his toes - es aren't ros - es, as

Moses - 3 - 1

could-n't be a lil-y or a daf-fy daf-fi-dil-ly. It's got to be a rose, 'cause it rhymes with 'Mose.'

Mo - ses,_____ Mo - ses,_____

Mo - ses._____

It's got to be a rose, 'cause it rhymes with 'Mose.'

# NEVER MET A MAN I DIDN'T LIKE

(from *The Will Rogers Follies*)

Music by
CY COLEMAN

Lyrics by
BETTY COMDEN and ADOLPH GREEN

Never Met a Man I Didn't Like - 8 - 1

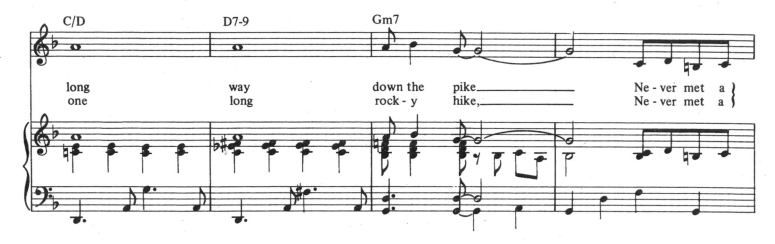

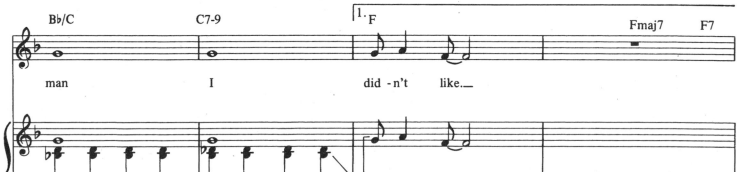

In all of my wand - rin', I've bumped in-to all\_\_ kinds of peo-ple;

Fan-cy ci - ne - ma stars,\_\_ fake ev - an - ge -lists, Pol-it - i - cians, Mor - ti -cians,

And I have reached the con-clu - sion, while hi - king the pike.\_\_

Though I try and I try,\_\_ nev - er once met a guy\_\_ that I did - n't like.\_\_ I said I've roamed a-long the

Na - pa Val - ley, Shu - bert Al - ley, Rue _____ de la Paix, _

O - kla - ho - ma and Ka - la - ma - zoo. _____

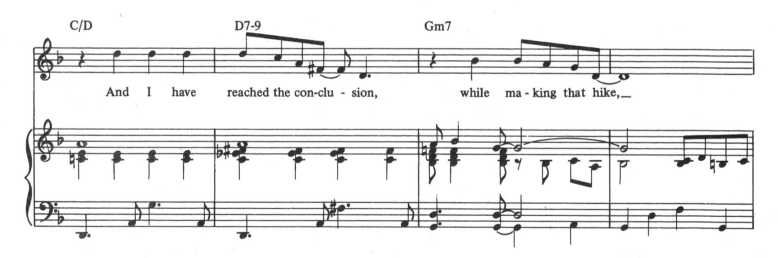

And I have reached the con-clu - sion, while ma - king that hike, _

Yes, I'll say till I'm done, _ No, I nev - er met one _ that I did - n't like. _

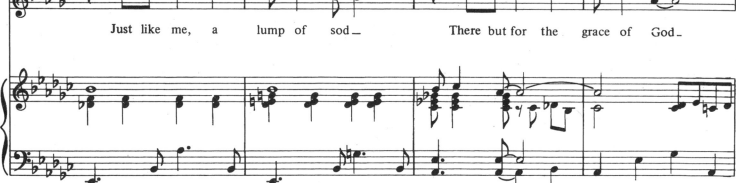

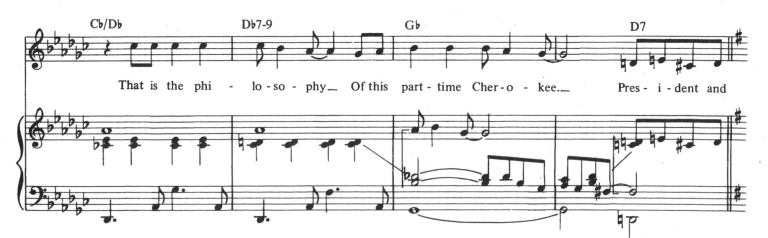

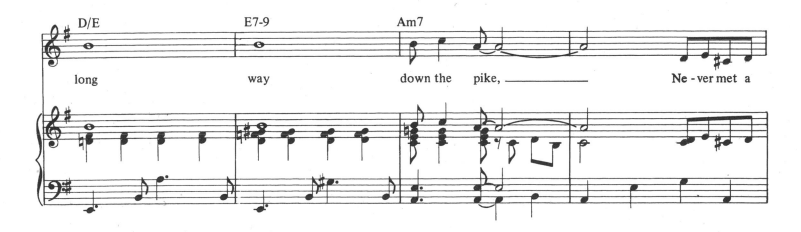

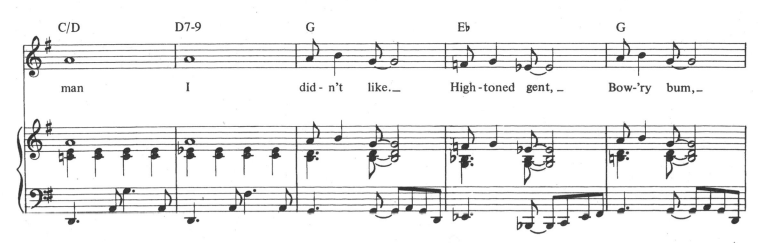

Never Met a Man I Didn't Like - 8 - 7

102

Prince of Wales.__ Work-ing Joe,__ Pat and Mike,__ Cher-o-kee,__ Phi-

lo-so-phy.__ Ne-ver met__ a man I did-n't like._____

Never Met a Man I Didn't Like - 8 - 8

# NEVER NEVER LAND

(from *Peter Pan*)

Lyrics by
BETTY COMDEN and ADOLPH GREEN

Music by
JULE STYNE

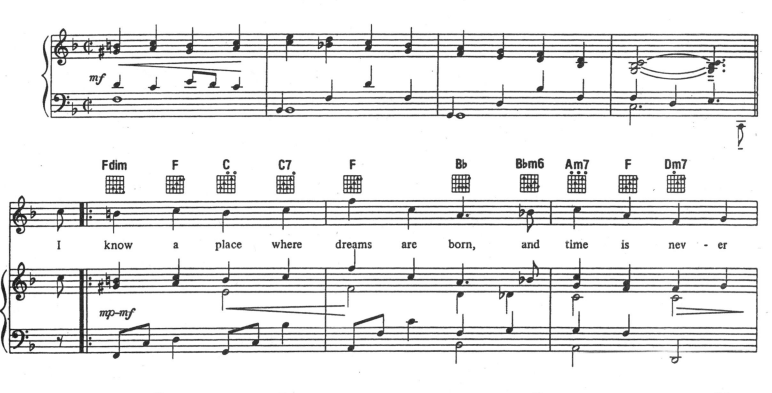

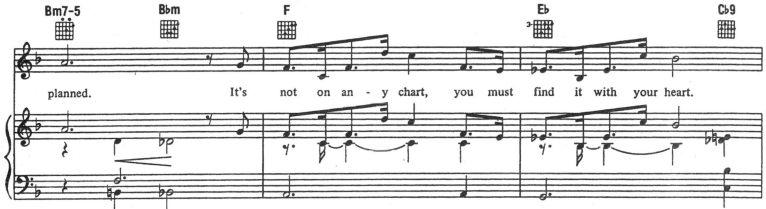

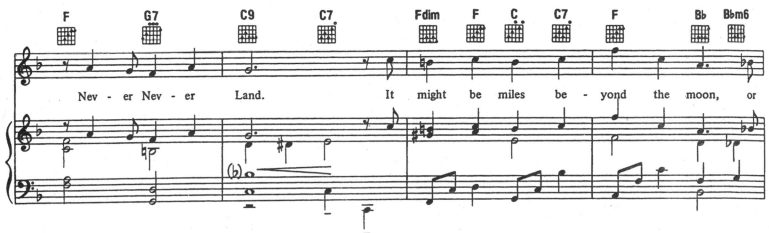

Never Never Land - 3 - 1

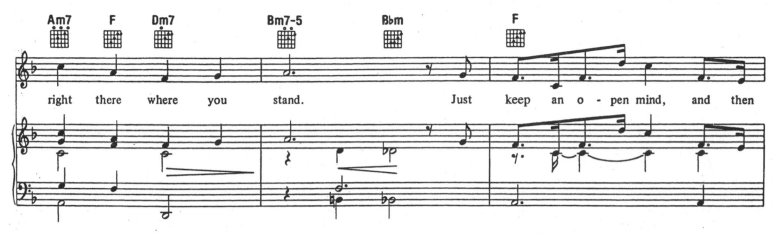

right there where you stand. Just keep an o-pen mind, and then

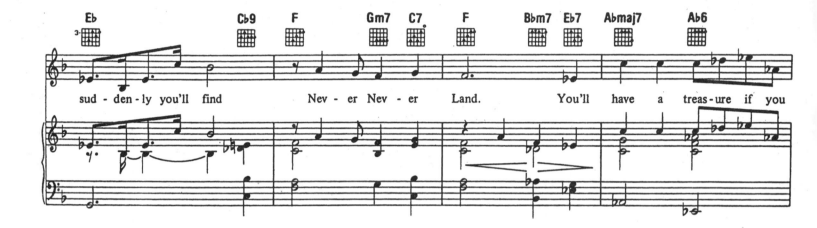

sud-den-ly you'll find Nev-er Nev-er Land. You'll have a treas-ure if you

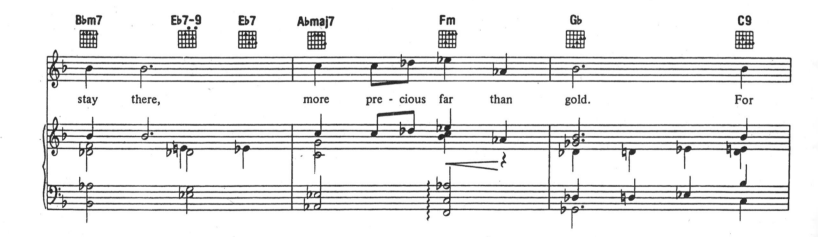

stay there, more pre-cious far than gold. For

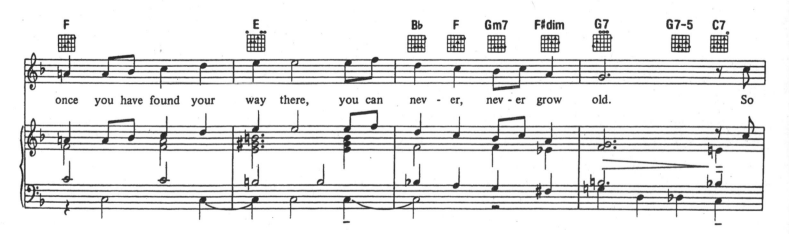

once you have found your way there, you can nev-er, nev-er grow old. So

105

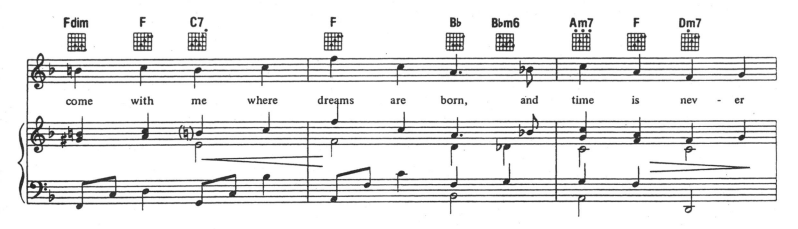

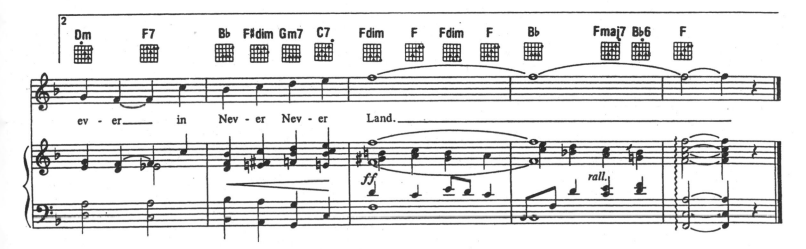

# OHIO

## (from *Wonderful Town*)

Lyrics by
**BETTY COMDEN** and **ADOLPH GREEN**

Music by
**LEONARD BERNSTEIN**

Ohio - 8 - 1

EILEEN:

out of the place,__ With Mom say-ing, "Ruth,__ what no date for this eve - ning? And

BOTH: RUTH:

Pop with, "Ei - leen,__ do be home, dear, by ten." Ugh! The

EILEEN:

gos - sip - y neigh-bors And eve - ry - one yap - ping who's go - ing with who,__ And

RUTH: EILEEN:

dat - ing those drips that I've known since I'm four.__ The Ki - wan - is Club Dance.. On the

111

Ohio - 8 - 6

EILEEN: *(in crying voice)*

Refrain: Why,_____ oh why,_____ oh why, oh,_____

RUTH: *(in crying voice)*

Why,_____ oh why,_____ oh why, oh,_____

Why did we ev - er leave O - hi - o?_____

Why did we ev - er leave O - hi - o?_____

Why did we fly, Why did we roam,

Why did we fly, Why did we roam,

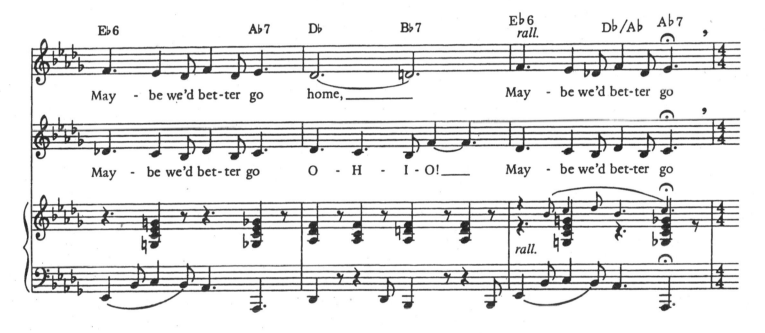

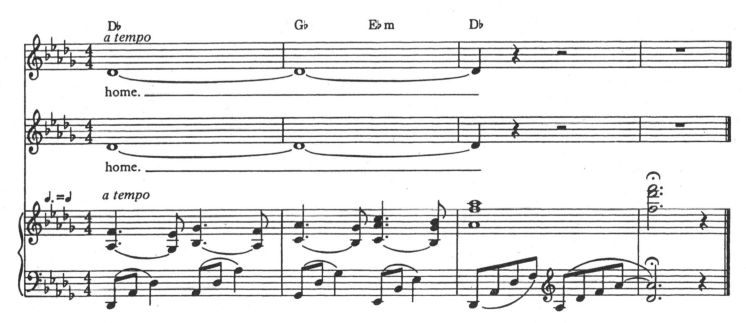

# NEW YORK, NEW YORK

## (from *On the Town*)

Lyrics by
BETTY COMDEN
and ADOLPH GREEN

Music by
LEONARD BERNSTEIN

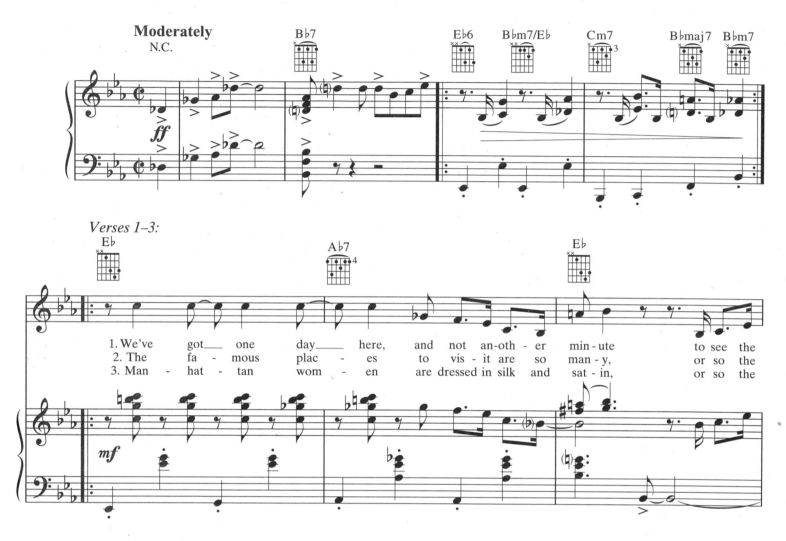

*Verses 1–3:*

1. We've got one day here, and not an-oth-er min-ute to see the fa-mous sights; we'll find the ro-mance and dan-ger wait-ing
2. The fa-mous plac-es to vis-it are so man-y, or so the guide-books say; I prom-ised dad-dy I would-n't miss on
3. Man-hat-tan wom-en are dressed in silk and sat-in, or so the fel-lows say; there's just one thing that's im-por-tant in Man-

New York, New York - 3 - 1

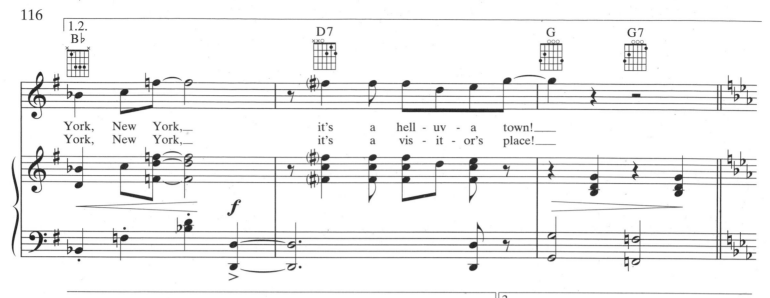

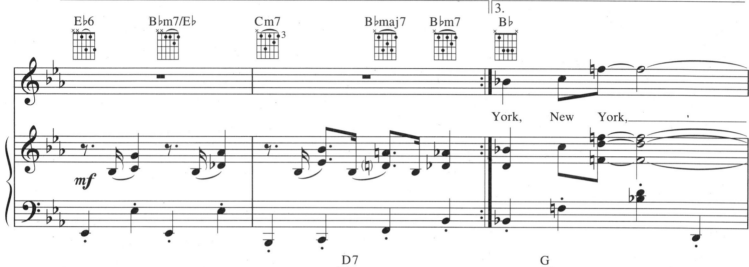

# ON THE TWENTIETH CENTURY

(from *On the Twentieth Century*)

Music by
CY COLEMAN

Lyrics by
BETTY COMDEN and ADOLPH GREEN

On the Twentieth Century - 10 - 1

122

On the Twentieth Century - 10 - 6

# THE PARTY'S OVER

## (from *Bells Are Ringing*)

Lyrics by
**BETTY COMDEN and ADOLPH GREEN**

Music by
**JULE STYNE**

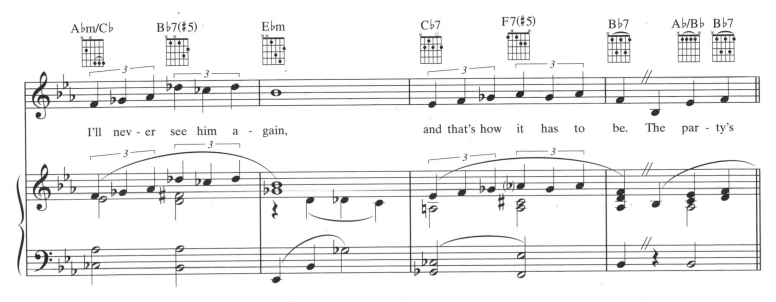

The Party's Over - 3 - 2

# SOME OTHER TIME
(from *On the Town*)

Lyrics by
BETTY COMDEN
and ADOLPH GREEN

Music by
LEONARD BERNSTEIN

**Freely, with sentiment ( ♩ = 96)**

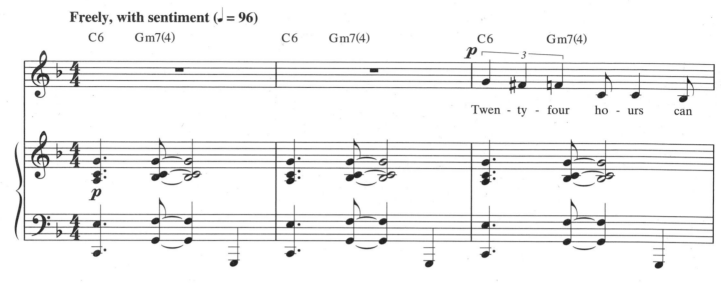

Twen-ty-four ho-urs can

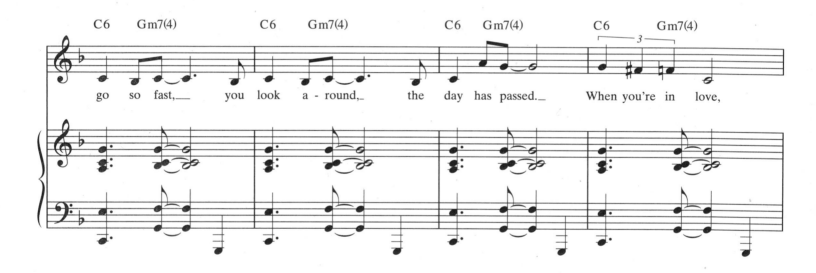

go so fast,___ you look a-round, the day has passed.___ When you're in love,

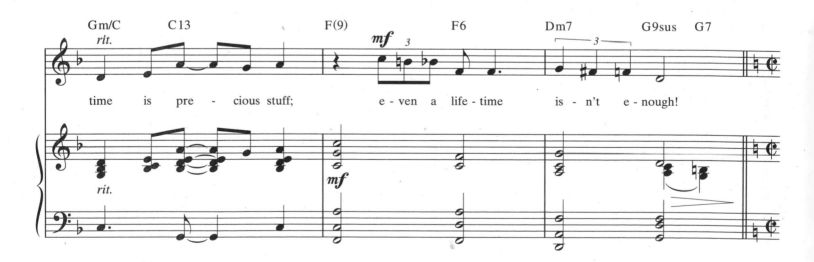

time is pre-cious stuff; e-ven a life-time is-n't e-nough!

Some Other Time - 6 - 1

Did-n't get half my wish - es, nev - er have seen you dry the dish - es.

Oh, well, we'll catch up some oth - er time.

Can't sat - is - fy my crav - ing, nev - er have watched you while you're shav - ing.

Oh, well, we'll catch up some oth - er time.

Just when the fun's be - gin - ning, comes the fi - nal

in - ning.

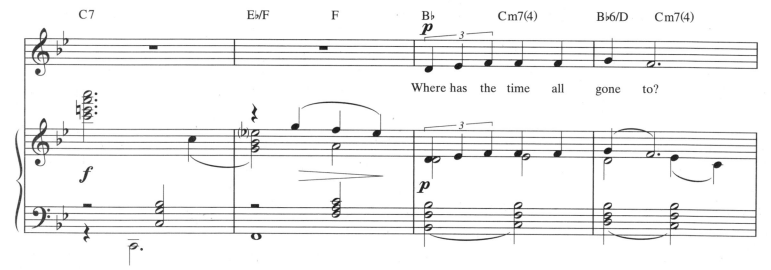

Where has the time all gone to?

Have - n't done half the things we want to. Oh, well...

# YOU MUSTN'T BE DISCOURAGED

(from *Fade Out–Fade In*)

Lyrics by
BETTY COMDEN and ADOLPH GREEN

Music by
JULE STYNE

**Moderately**

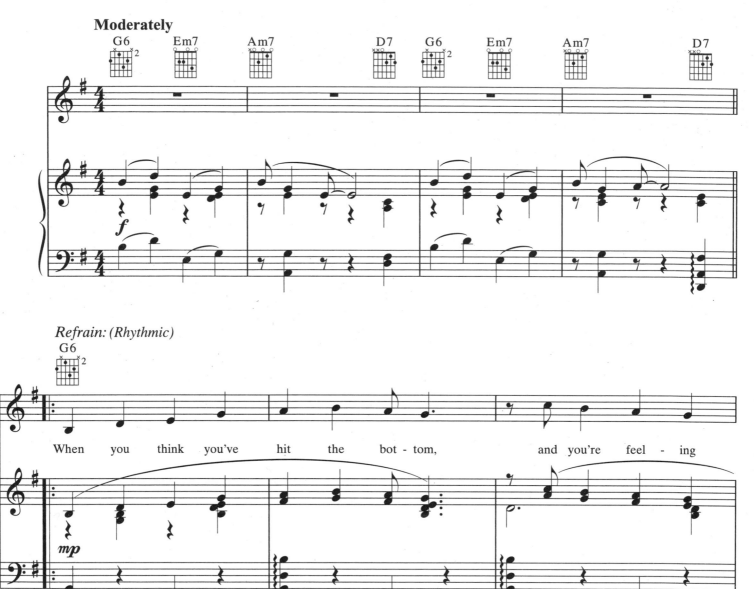

*Refrain: (Rhythmic)*

When you think you've hit the bot-tom, and you're feel-ing

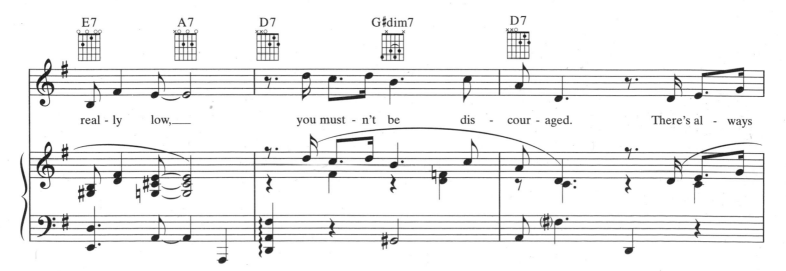

real-ly low,___ you must-n't be dis-cour-aged. There's al-ways

You Mustn't Be Discouraged - 4 - 1

one step fur - ther down___ you can go.___

When you're ly - ing in the gut - ter,

feel - ing just a bit un - sure,___ just wait un - til to -

mor - row, you may be ly - ing flat, face down___ in a sewer.___

# WHEN THE WEATHER'S BETTER

(from *Hallelujah, Baby!*)

Lyrics by
BETTY COMDEN and ADOLPH GREEN

Music by
JULE STYNE

When the___ sun is high-er and when the___ streets are dri-er, yes, when the___ weath-er's bet-ter, we'll get to-geth-er, you and me.___ But look a-round, my

When the Weather's Better - 5 - 1

143

When the Weather's Better - 5 - 4